Parenting Struggles?

Don Barnes

Published by Don Barnes, 2024.

This publication provides the Author's opinion and neither the publisher nor the author intends to render legal, accounting, or other professional advice with this publication.
The publisher and the author disclaim any personal liability, loss or risk incurred as a consequence of the use and application, directly or indirectly, of advice, information or methods presented in this publication.
First Edition

Copyright © 2025

By Don Barnes / Tryune Works!

TRYUNE WORKS! and Life works in threes are trademarks and copyrights of Don Barnes and Tryune Works!

 **LifeWorksInThrees.com**

All rights reserved. No part of this manuscript may be reproduced (by any means) without the expressed written permission of Don Barnes and Tryune Works!

About the Author

Don is the founder and author of Life Works in Threes!™ E-books. He is a lifelong Texan who has traveled extensively while taking a keen interest in human behavior. His curiosity about life and what drives humans led him to the discovery of how life works in threes. He coined this term as the *Tryune Concept.*

Don attended college on an athletic scholarship and then embarked on a 30-year career in the oil and gas industry. Since the year 2000, he has been a consultant for distributors and manufacturers of various industries. Along the way, he worked on his Tryune discovery in hopes of someday sharing his findings with those struggling unnecessarily... in life. What Don surmised from 40+ years of R&D was that people were struggling unnecessarily because they were not aware that "life works in threes." They, for the most part, have been living their lives <u>by chance</u> rather than <u>by choice,</u> he also discovered.

From this, he began focusing on the "mechanics of life" which shows formulas for success with subjects such as *life, health, money, purpose and so forth.* When people are able to grasp the Tryune Concept, they can apply the formulas with topics that interest them and begin eliminating the struggle. This epiphany is what triggered his Tryune venture and is now on the path of sharing with all who desire to improve on their lives.

Don currently resides in Southern California and Texas while overseeing his businesses and investments.

Life Works in Threes™

When I was a kid growing up, no one sat me down and said, "Okay Don, I'm going to show you how life works so that you can navigate your way through adulthood." I graduated from school, got married and went about my way with the "learn as you go" concept. It was kind of like putting together a backyard swing set without a set of instructions. Lots of frustration and do-overs, for sure!

My discovery of the "triune" word and noticing how things come together in threes is really what set me off on researching that maybe "life comes in three" ...sort of a mechanical approach to managing life, if you will. I combed the libraries and bookstores for information on this and found one book on the subject that was written back in 1951. The author's name was John S. Arant.

What Mr. Arant had to say is this "For lack of a better name, I have called this *The Triangle of Triumph* and therefore, consistent with the name, since most of these conclusions are built on the geometric figure of the triangle." He continued "All Life and all lives are seated in, and circumscribed by, the triangle. The Author and Source and Director of all life is Himself triune in character – Father, Son, and Holy Spirit. Man is of triple nature – body, mind, and spirit – and within those three there are many triangles – desires, development, decay; intellect, will, sensibilities. Of this "paced interlude in the midst of eternity" which we call time there is the triangle of Past, Present, and Future. Space – that limitless and measureless element of the physical universe – is best known in terms of Height, Breadth, and Depth. Try building yourself some triangles along the lines of your Will, your Work, your Way – You will find some interesting angles.

So, for the first time, I realized that life is designed in a mechanical way to come in threes. That means you don't have to rely on wishing and hoping things turn out okay. You can actually look at the three parts that a particular thing is made of and then apply them to get what you're wanting. Like a three-ingredient recipe or a combination lock. With a combination lock, you need the three exact numbers to unlock the lock...otherwise you will continue to struggle.

Some 40 years later, I accumulated things that work in threes and that's when I knew I needed to share this with anyone wanting answers. To have success/harmony in your life, just apply the three parts of an area you're working on, and things will fall into place. I also learned that the recipe for success with just about anything is by doing these three things, consistently – THINK positively, SPEAK positively and ACT positively. For example, if I want to be a successful artist. I would think to myself "I can do this because I have the talent." Then I would speak it this way "Yes, I am working on my art degree and plan to do portraits professionally." Finally, I would act on that by taking art classes and continue crafting my skill. Eventually, I will see the positive results/success I'm looking for.

Conversely, if I think positively but speak negatively...it will cancel out. Or if I speak positively but have no positive action going on...nothing will happen.

I looked up "How Life Works" and "The Mechanics of Life" and these are really talking about the biology of how our cells work and other chemistry. Life Works in Threes! teaches that life is kind of like building blocks. Pick a topic you may be struggling with. See the three parts that topic consists of and then start applying them...on a consistent basis. That will help you overcome the struggle and get you back in harmony/success with how life works.

For 30+ years I was a golf instructor (by accident). My two kids had some success playing junior golf and so friends and neighbors would ask me to show them and their kids how to play golf successfully. From all of this, I got pretty good at watching golfers on the driving range and could spot right away why they were struggling with hitting bad golf shots. I was able to do that because I knew the three steps to hitting good golf shots. I learned them from studying golf and played for several decades. I "broke the code" for me so to speak.

So now you know that life works in threes. You can live your life *by choice* rather than *by chance* and that my friend... is the key to a fulfilling life.

LIFE WORKS
IN THREES!

My sanctuary on the Pacific coast

Introduction

Being a parent is a remarkable journey filled with countless privileges that often sneak up on you when you least expect it. One of the greatest privileges is witnessing the world through the innocent eyes of your child. Whether it's marveling at the wonders of nature during a simple walk in the park or seeing their uncontainable joy over the smallest achievements, being a parent offers a front-row seat to some of life's most precious moments. It's like having a backstage pass to the show of life, where you get to experience the purest forms of love, curiosity, and wonder.

Another privilege of parenthood is the opportunity for personal growth and learning. Your child becomes your greatest teacher, constantly challenging you to be the best version of yourself. From mastering patience during late-night feedings to finding creative solutions to everyday problems, being a parent pushes you beyond your limits and helps you discover strengths you never knew you had. There's something profoundly humbling about realizing that you have the power to shape another human being's life, and it's a privilege that comes with immense responsibility but also immense reward.

But perhaps the most profound privilege of all is the unconditional love that flows between parent and child. It's a bond unlike any other, forged through countless cuddles, laughter, tears, and shared experiences. Knowing that you are someone's everything, their safe haven in a chaotic world, is both humbling and empowering. And as you watch your child grow and flourish, you realize that the true privilege of parenthood lies in the opportunity to leave a lasting legacy of love, kindness, and strength for generations to come.

My discovery of the Tryune Concept

Before we dive into parenting struggles and how to overcome them, let me share my discovery of the Tryune Concept and how life works in threes. It all began in the summer of 1982.

I grew up with parents who treated everyone with decency and respect. My three older sisters and I were raised in a home that was "middle-class traditional." We lived in modest homes in different small towns, attended school and church on a regular basis and celebrated all the traditional holidays. Eventually we settled during the spring of 1964 in the big city of Houston, Texas. I'll never forget the vastness of the city and hearing sirens from police cars, fire trucks and ambulances on a regular basis. I was excited and scared at the same time.

Once settled in this fast-paced city, I finished my growing-up years with an academic diploma and sweetheart intact. I got a job, bought a car, got married, bought a house and produced two beautiful babies in a span of about 5 years. Talk about having to grow up fast!

Things went from great in my childhood to absolute misery in my young adulthood. I began to struggle with my job because deep down I just hated what I was doing. This problem created a snowball effect because soon after, my weight, my finances, my relationships, my happiness and everything else worth saving was going down the drain. I eventually hit a level of frustration that I had never experienced before and didn't know how to get out of it. My cry for help was for anyone or anything to come to my rescue. I just ran out of solutions for my situation.

This is when my discovery happened.

One night shortly after my meltdown, while sleeping soundly, the word "triune" began to softly pound in my head like a mantra. I woke up a little startled and decided to go look up the word in my favorite dictionary (this was WAY before Google.) The definition said '**triune** (try-une) – 1) a group of three things; united. 2) Being 3 in 1 such as *humans are mental, physical and spiritual.* I scratched my head, got a glass of water and went back to bed.

The next day while driving around town, I began thinking about things that I was taught in my younger years that came in threes. My Boy Scout manual taught that to have **character**, I needed to be *1) physically strong, 2) mentally awake and 3) morally straight.* My high school football coach would say emphatically "If you want to be **a good football player**, you have to be *1) mobile 2) agile and 3) hostile!*" My first sales manager shared with me that to be **a successful salesman**, I needed to have *1) sales skills, 2) product knowledge and 3) a good image.*

"Hmm", I thought, "wonder if there are other examples out there of things that work in threes?" So, some 40 years later, I have researched and discovered that many, many things work in threes. What this message was telling me is that to achieve success or balance in any significant area of my life, the three things that area consisted of had to be present continuously. That's when I had my epiphany. This discovery was telling me the secret to how life <u>really</u> works.

Tryune is a play on the word "triune" as an invitation to "try" this concept. Furthermore, we do not say that life <u>only</u> works in threes. Life also works in ones, twos, fours and so on. What has been observed though is that the many things significant to life, just so happen to come and work in threes. That's what is being shared in this book.

Now, you are about to see 40+ years of research and proof that life works in threes. I did not make up any of these topics. I invite you to research them on the internet to validate what is written here. There are some interesting facts that most of us have never realized...until now.

How Life Works in Threes (around 200 examples)

<u>LIFE</u>

Humans consist of *body, mind and soul.*

A human's basic needs are *health, income and provisions.*

A human's basic wants are *comfort, gain and approval.*

Our minds are made up of the *conscious, the subconscious and the unconscious.*

Philosophy explains *the id, the ego and superego.*

Atoms consist of *protons, neutrons and electrons.*

Motion is explained by *three basic laws.*

Science falls under three main branches: *natural, social and formal sciences*

Time is *past, present and future*...at the same time.

Electricity consists of *ohms, amperes and voltage.*

Music's basic elements are *duration, pitch and timbre.*

Democracy is a government *of the people, by the people and for the people.*

U.S. branches of government are *the judicial, the executive and the legislative.*

Armed Forces protect us on *land, air and sea.*

Environmentally, we are asked *to reduce, recycle and re-use.*

The news program gives us *the news, sports and conditions.*

Our days consist of *morning, afternoon and evening.*

Three months in each season of the year

Our main meals are known as *breakfast, lunch and dinner.*

A balanced diet consists of *good proteins, carbohydrates and fats.*

Traditional Family consists of *father, mother, and child(ren)*

<u>SCIENCES</u>

Three major branches of natural science – *(physical, earth/ space and life sciences)*

Three major branches of modern physics - *(classical, relativistic, quantum)*

Three major branches of biology *(botany, zoology, microbiology)*

Three spatial dimensions: *height* (up/down), *width* (left/ right) and *depth* (forwards/backwards)

Three-gauge bosons (photon, gluon, W&Z bosons)

Three types of elementary particles *(leptons, quarks, gauge bosons)*

Three quarks in every proton *(two "up" and one "down")*

Three primary colors of light *(red, green, blue)*

Three color tone properties *(hue, value, chroma)*

Three laws of motion (*Newton's laws*)

Three laws of planetary motion (*Kepler's laws*)

Three layers of the Sun's interior (*core, radiative zone, convective zone*)

Three layers of the Sun's atmosphere (*photosphere, chromosphere, corona*)

Three types of meteorites (*iron, stony iron, stony*)

Three types of galaxy shapes (*elliptical, spiral, irregular*)

Three substances of the universe (*normal matter, 'dark matter', 'dark energy'*)

Three phases of the moon (*new moon, first quarter, full moon*)

Three planetary regions (*temperate, sub-tropical, tropical*)

Three layers of the Earth (*crust, mantle, core*)

Three components of an ecosystem (*producers, consumers, decomposers*)

Three types of rocks (*igneous, sedimentary, metamorphic*)

Three types of fossil fuels (*coal, crude oil, natural gas*)

Three hydrological processes (*evaporation, condensation, precipitation*)

Three basic types of (meteorological) precipitation (*liquid, freezing, frozen*)

Three types of substances *(mono-constituent, multi-constituent, UVCB)*

Three phases of (normal) matter *(solid, liquid, gas)*

Three types of covalent chemical bonds *(single, double and triple bonds)*

Three isotopes of hydrogen *(protium, deuterium, tritium)*

Three atoms in each molecule of water *(two hydrogen atoms and an oxygen atom)*

Three endings to salts *(-ide, -ite, -ate)*

Three requirements for fire *(fuel, oxygen, heat)*

Three nucleotide bases in a genetic codon

Three domains of life *(archaea, bacteria and eukaryotes)*

Three major groups of flowering plants *(monocots, eudicots, magnolids)*

Three major functions that are basic to plant growth and development: *(photosynthesis* [making sugars], *respiration* [metabolizing those sugars], and *transpiration* [water vapor loss]

Three things that the chlorophyll in plants needs for photosynthesis to take place: *(sunlight, carbon dioxide and water)*

Transpiration serves three roles: *(cooling the plant, moving minerals* and *sugars through the plant,* and *maintaining the turgidity pressure* [stiffness] *of the plant's cells)*

Three parts of an insect's body *(head, thorax, abdomen)*

BIOLOGY

Three types of cones in the retina, relating to the three primary colors

Three semi-circular canals in the ear *(lateral, anterior, posterior)*

Three sections in the ear *(outer, middle, inner)*

Three ossicles in the middle ear *(malleus, incus, stapes)*

Three segments to each limb *(proximal, mid, distal)*

Three bones in each arm *(humerus, radius, ulna)*

Three joints in the arm *(shoulder, elbow, wrist)*

Three joints in the leg *(hip, knee, ankle)*

Three joints in the elbow *(humeroulnar, humeroradial, proximal radioulnar)*

Three functional compartments in the knee joint *(the femoropatellar, medial femorotibial* and *lateral femorotibial articulations)*

Three types of fibrous joints *(sutures, gomphoses, syndesmoses)*

Three types of bone in each hand (*carpals, metacarpals, phalanges*)

Three types of bone in each foot (*tarsals, metatarsals, phalanges*)

Three bones (phalanges) in each finger and in each toe (*proximal, intermediate, distal*)

Three layers of skin (*dermis, epidermis, hypodermis*)

Three components of a cell (*cell membrane, nucleus, cytoplasm*)

Three types of blood vessels (*arteries, veins, capillaries*)

Three types of blood cells [*red* (erythrocytes), *white* (leukocytes), *platelets* (thrombocytes)]

Three processes of the intestinal tract (*ingestion, digestion, excretion*)

Three germ layers (*Endoderm, Mesoderm, Ectoderm*)

Three parts of a human tooth (*crown, neck, root*)

Three organs of otolaryngology (*ear, nose, throat*)

Three major body systems (*digestive, circulatory, respiratory*)

Three parts to a neuron: (*soma* [*cell body*], *axon, dendrites*)

Three main parts of the brain (*forebrain, midbrain, hindbrain*)

Three parts of the forebrain (*cerebrum, thalamus, hypothalamus*)

Three parts of the midbrain (*colliculi, tegmentum, cerebral peduncles*)

Three parts of the hindbrain (*cerebellum, pons, medulla*)

Three membranes enclosing the brain (*dura mater, arachnoid, pia mater*)

The brain operates on three levels: *consciously* (for cognitive thought and declarative memory); *subconsciously* (for pre-planned actions and procedural memory); and *unconsciously* (for breathing, heart beating, etc.)

Our conscious mind is fed from three sources: *our senses* (which can be fooled); *our memory* (which is flawed); and *our imagination* (which is inventive)

Three aspects of the human mind (*memory, intellect, will*)

Three parts of the human personality (*id, ego, superego*)

The sum of human capacity consists of three abilities (*thought, word and deed*)

Three times of man (*birth, life, death*)

Three periods of the Gait Cycle (*initial double limb support, single limb support, and terminal double limb support*)

MUSIC

Three types of musical notes (*sharps, flats, naturals*)

Three aspects of a song (*lyrics, melody, rhythm*)

Three types of musical chords (*root, third, fifth*)

<u>MATHEMATICS</u>

Three types of a real number (*positive, negative, zero*)

Three parts to any arithmetic operation: for addition: *augend, addend and sum* - for subtraction: *minuend, subtrahend and difference* - for multiplication: *multiplicand, multiplier and product* - for division: *dividend, divisor and quotient*

Three laws of arithmetic operations (*commutative, associative, distributive*)

Three types of equivalence relation (*reflexivity, symmetry, transitivity*)

Three types of symmetry operations (*translation, rotation, reflection*)

Three geometries (*Euclidean, spherical, hyperbolic*)

The number 3 is the basis of an entire branch of mathematics, called trigonometry (from the Greek *trigonon* "triangle" + *metron* "measure")

Three trigonometric functions (*sine, cosine, tangent*)

Three types of average (*mean, mode, median*)

<u>GRAMMAR</u>

Three logical operators (*AND, OR and NOT*)

Three laws of logic (*identity, noncontradiction, excluded middle*)

Three parts of a logical syllogism (*major premise, minor premise, conclusion*)

Three grammatical parts to a sentence (*subject, verb, complement*)

Three persons in grammar [*1st person* (I/we), *2nd* (you or your), *3rd* (he/she/it/they)]

Three genders in grammar [*masculine* (he/him), *feminine* (she/her), *neuter* (it)]

Three forms of comparison in grammar [*positive, comparative* (more, -er), *superlative* (most, -est)]

Three cases in (English) grammar [*subjective/nominative* (he), *objective/accusative* (him) and *possessive/genitive* (his)]

Three parts of a narrative (*beginning, middle, end*)

Components of an essay (*introduction, body, conclusion*)

Elements of a rhetorical appeal (*ethos, pathos, logos*)

Aspects of a story (*plot, characters, setting*)

RELIGION

The Creator – *omniscient, omnipotent, omnipresent*

Christian God – *Father, Son, Holy Spirit*

Jesus – *The Way, The Truth, The Life*

Ancient Near East- *Qudshu, Astarte, Anat*

Classical Antiquity – Many dieties came in threes

Hinduism – Para Brahman is *Brahma, Visnu, Shiva*

Ancient Celtic Cultures – *many example of triad dieties*

Buddhism – *The three jewels*

Taoism – *The three pure ones*

Islam – *Fear, Hope and Love*

Baha'i - *Intention, Power and Action*

Confucianism – *Benevolence, Wisdom and Courage*

OTHER TRIUNE EXAMPLES

3 Coins in a Fountain

3 Days of the Condor

3 Miles in a League

3 Goals in a Hat Trick

3 Piece Suit

3 Feet in a Yard

3 Books in Lord of the Rings

3 Ring Circus

3 Ships of Christopher Columbus

3 Sheets to the Wind

3 Books in a Trilogy

3 Wheels on a Tricycle

3 Wise Men

3-Legged Race

3 Ring Circus

3-Wheeler

3 Cornered Hat

3 Dimensional

3 Musketeers

3 R's (reading, 'riting, 'rithmatic)

3 Sides of a triangle

3 Races in the Triple Crown (horse racing)

3 Angles in a Triangle

3 Trimesters in a Pregnancy

3 Flavors in Neapolitan Ice Cream

3 Stars in Orion's belt

3 Barleycorns in an Inch

3 Hands on a Clock (with the Seconds Hand)

3 Colors in a Flag

3 Minute Egg

3 Great Pyramids at Giza

3 Holes in a Bowling Ball

3 Colors in a Set of Traffic Lights

3 Minutes in a Boxing Round

3 Teaspoons in a Tablespoon

3 Legs on a Stool

3 Monastic Vows (Obience, Stability, Conversatio Morum)

3 Body Types: Endomorph, Mesomorph, Ectomorph

3 Ring Notebooks

3 Germ layers: Endoderm, Mesoderm, Ectoderm

3 Species of Homo: Homo habilis, Homo erectus, Homo sapiens

3 Basic parts of a camera: Lens, Shutter, Sensor

3 Stages of a Project lifecycle: initiation, planning, execution

The Truth, The Whole Truth and Nothing but the Truth

Life, Liberty and the Pursuit of Happiness

Hear no Evil, See no Evil, Speak no Evil

National motto of France/Haiti: Liberty, Equality, Fraternity

Paper, Rock, Scissors

Ready, Aim, Fire

On Your mark, Get Set, Go

Olympic medals of gold, silver, bronze

Types of joints (ball & socket, hinge, pivot)

Stages of a rocket launch (launch, orbit, re-entry)

Parts of a joke (setup, delivery, punchline)

Primary components of a transistor (emitter, base, collector)

Primary components of an airplane (fuselage, wings, empennage)

Basic components of a computer: CPU, memory, storage

Three phases in the development of technology (*eotechnic* [*mechanical*], *paleotechnic* [*steam-powered*] and *neotechnic* [*electric-powered*]

Communication systems require three components (*transmitter, channel, receiver*)

The list goes on. See if you can find more examples as they are everywhere in our universe! Now that you know that life works in threes (with proof!), we can begin to apply this concept to whatever topics we want.

So, to overcome struggles in parenting, we need to apply the three areas that parenting consist of – FOUNDATION, FOSTER, PREPARE. Let's get started!

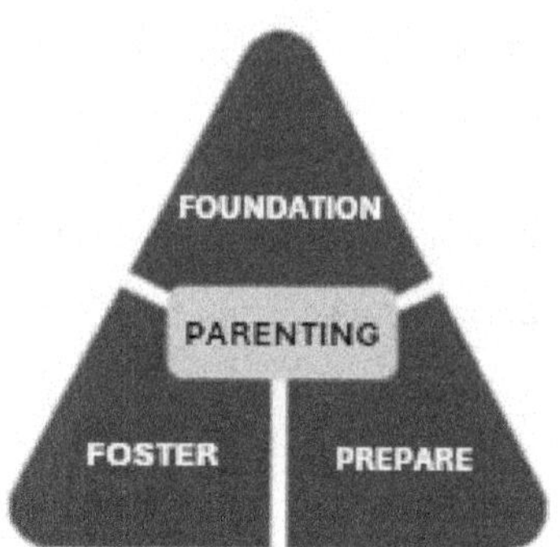
FOUNDATION
PARENTING
FOSTER
PREPARE

PARENTING

Parenting is no small feat—it's a journey filled with countless responsibilities and joys. One of the most fundamental duties parents have is to provide a nurturing environment where their children can grow and thrive. This goes beyond just meeting physical needs; it encompasses emotional support, guidance through life's challenges, and fostering a sense of security. From the moment a child is born, parents are entrusted with the incredible task of shaping their development and character.

Central to parenting is the role of being a role model. Children learn by observing and imitating their parents, so it's crucial for parents to embody the values and behaviors they wish to instill in their children. Whether it's displaying kindness, resilience, or perseverance in the face of adversity, parents serve as the first and most influential teachers in a child's life. This duty extends to teaching important life skills, such as empathy, respect for others, and the ability to make responsible decisions.

Today, parents are tasked with providing education and preparing their children for the complexities of the world. This includes not only formal education but also imparting practical knowledge and wisdom gained from experience. From teaching basic life skills like cooking and managing finances to discussing important topics such as ethics, relationships, and personal responsibility, parents play a vital role in preparing their children to become independent and capable adults. Ultimately, the duty of parents in the upbringing of their children is a profound commitment that shapes the future generation and contributes to building a better society.

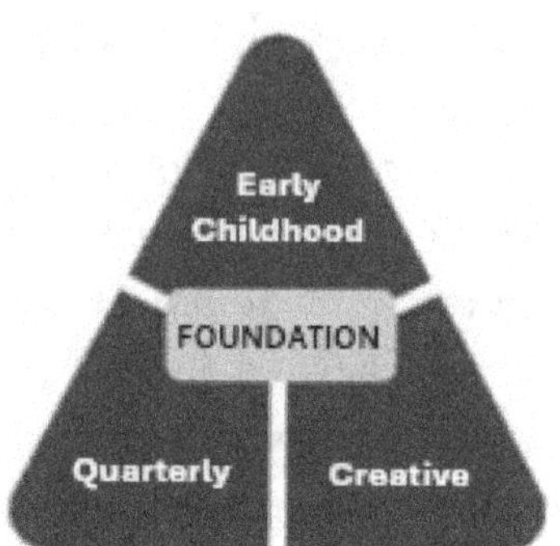

Early
Childhood
FOUNDATION
Quarterly
Creative

FOUNDATION

Parenting is a huge undertaking that begins with laying the foundation for success during childhood. This is what it looks like in a nutshell:

1. **Early Childhood (0-6 years)**: This stage is characterized by rapid physical, cognitive, and socio-emotional development. Infancy (0-2 years) is marked by significant growth and motor development, as well as the emergence of basic language skills and attachment to caregivers. The preschool period (3-6 years) is a time of exploration and discovery, as children develop language fluency, social skills, and basic cognitive abilities such as memory, problem-solving, and creativity. Play becomes a central activity, facilitating learning and socialization, while parental guidance and support play a critical role in shaping children's values, beliefs, and behaviors.

2. **Middle Childhood (6-12 years)**: This stage is characterized by continued growth and development across multiple domains, including physical, cognitive, social, and emotional areas. School-age children experience significant cognitive advances, including improvements in memory, attention, and reasoning skills, as well as the development of a more sophisticated understanding of concepts such as time, space, and cause-and-effect relationships. Socially, children begin to form more complex peer relationships, navigate group dynamics, and develop a sense of identity and self-esteem. Emotionally, they may experience increased independence and autonomy, as well as challenges related to self-regulation and coping with stress.

3. **Adolescence (12-18 years)**: This stage marks the transition from childhood to adulthood and is characterized by significant physical, cognitive, emotional, and social changes. Puberty initiates rapid physical growth and sexual maturation,

accompanied by hormonal changes that impact mood, behavior, and identity formation. Adolescents experience cognitive advances in abstract thinking, moral reasoning, and decision-making, as well as increased autonomy and independence from parents. Socially, they navigate peer relationships, romantic interests, and societal expectations, while grappling with questions of identity, values, and future aspirations. Emotional challenges such as mood swings, risk-taking behavior, and peer pressure are common during this period, as adolescents strive to establish a sense of self and find their place in the world.

These stages of childhood are fluid and overlapping, and individual development can vary widely based on factors such as genetics, environment, culture, and personal experiences. However, understanding these general stages can help parents, caregivers, and educators provide appropriate support and guidance to children as they navigate the complexities of growing up.

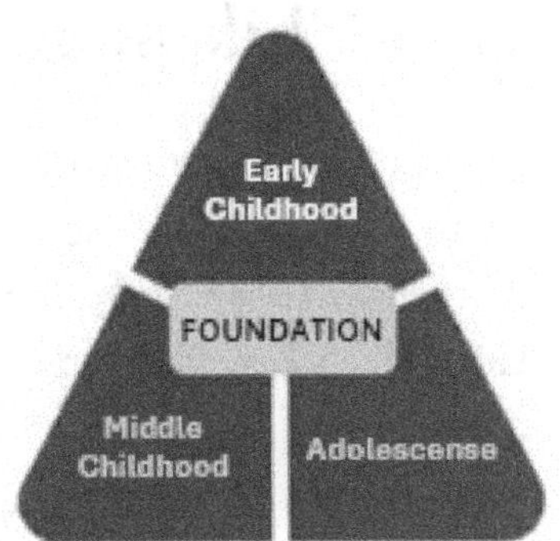
Early
Childhood
FOUNDATION
Middle
Childhood
Adolescense

Early Childhood

Parenting during the early years of childhood is like navigating through a delightful maze filled with surprises, challenges, and an abundance of love. It's a time of wonderment, where every day brings new discoveries and milestones. From those first tentative steps to the sweet sound of their first words, these moments shape the foundation of their future selves. As parents, our role is akin to being the gentle guides in this incredible journey, providing support, encouragement, and plenty of cuddles along the way.

One of the most magical aspects of parenting young children is witnessing their boundless curiosity and insatiable thirst for knowledge. From asking "why" a million times to exploring the world with wide-eyed wonder, their enthusiasm is infectious. As parents, we have the privilege of nurturing this curiosity by fostering an environment that encourages exploration and experimentation. Whether it's through play, storytelling, or hands-on activities, every interaction becomes an opportunity for learning and growth.

But amidst the joy and wonder of parenting young children, there are also moments of uncertainty and doubt. From sleepless nights to temper tantrums, the journey can sometimes feel like riding a rollercoaster of emotions. Yet, it's in these challenging moments that we discover our resilience as parents and the depth of our unconditional love. By embracing both the highs and lows with patience and understanding, we not only nurture our children's development but also cultivate a strong bond built on trust and empathy. So, let's cherish every precious moment, knowing that in the end, it's the journey itself that truly matters.

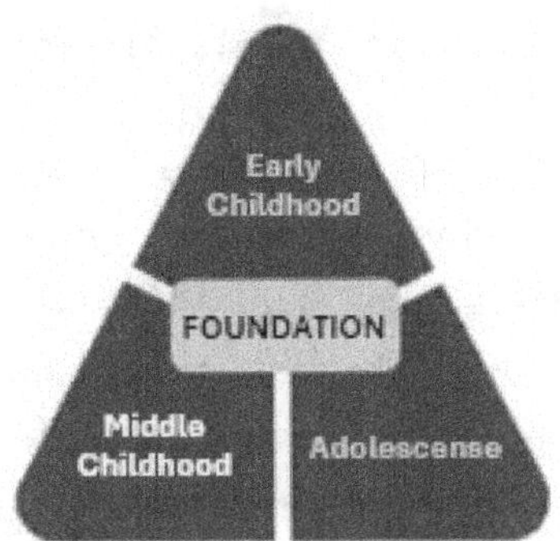
Early
Childhood
FOUNDATION
Middle
Childhood
Adolescense

Middle Childhood

Entering the realm of middle childhood is like embarking on a new adventure filled with exploration, growth, and a sprinkle of mischief. During these years, our children are like little sponges, eagerly soaking up knowledge and experiences from the world around them. As parents, our role evolves into that of a supportive coach, guiding them through the ups and downs of this exciting phase of development.

One of the joys of parenting during middle childhood is witnessing our children's blossoming independence and burgeoning sense of self. From mastering new skills to forming their own opinions and interests, they begin to carve out their unique identities. As parents, we have the privilege of fostering their autonomy while providing a safety net of love and guidance. Whether it's cheering them on from the sidelines of the soccer field or listening attentively to their imaginative tales, every moment spent nurturing their independence strengthens our bond and fills our hearts with pride.

Yet, amidst the newfound independence, middle childhood also brings its own set of challenges. From navigating friendships to facing academic pressures, our children are constantly learning to navigate the complexities of the world around them. As parents, we play a vital role in providing them with the tools they need to overcome obstacles and thrive. Through open communication, empathy, and a sprinkle of humor, we help them develop resilience and confidence in themselves. Together, we embark on this journey of discovery, celebrating their triumphs and comforting them through their setbacks, knowing that every experience is a valuable lesson in shaping their bright futures.

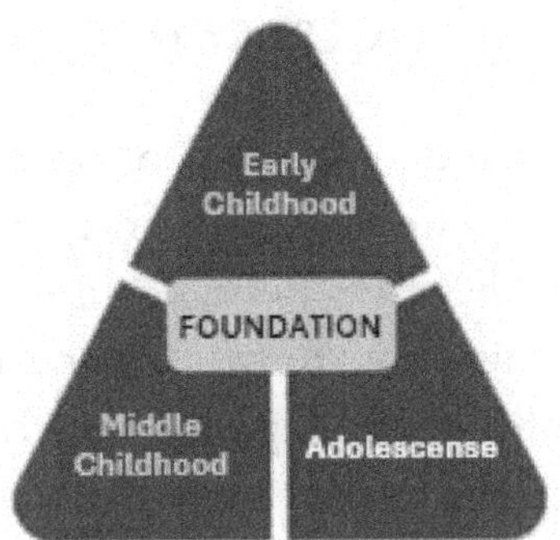

Early
Childhood
FOUNDATION
Middle
Childhood
Adolescense

Adolescence

Ah, adolescence—the rollercoaster ride of hormones, emotions, and self-discovery! Parenting during these transformative years is like navigating through uncharted waters, where every wave brings new challenges and opportunities for growth. As our children transition from childhood to adulthood, our role as parents evolves into that of a trusted confidant and guiding light, offering support, understanding, and plenty of patience along the way.

One of the most exciting aspects of parenting adolescents is witnessing their journey of self-discovery and personal growth. From exploring their passions to challenging societal norms, they embark on a quest to find their place in the world. As parents, we have the privilege of walking alongside them on this journey, providing a safe harbor amidst the storm of uncertainty. Whether it's late-night heart-to-heart conversations or cheering them on from the sidelines of their first job or school play, every moment spent together strengthens the bond between parent and child.

Yet, adolescence also comes with its fair share of trials and tribulations. From mood swings to identity crises, our children navigate a myriad of challenges as they strive to find their footing in a complex world. As parents, we offer a steady hand and a compassionate ear, ready to lend support and guidance whenever needed. Through open communication, mutual respect, and a healthy dose of humor, we weather the storms of adolescence together, emerging stronger and closer than ever before. Together, we embrace the journey of adolescence, knowing that every stumble and triumph is a steppingstone towards adulthood.

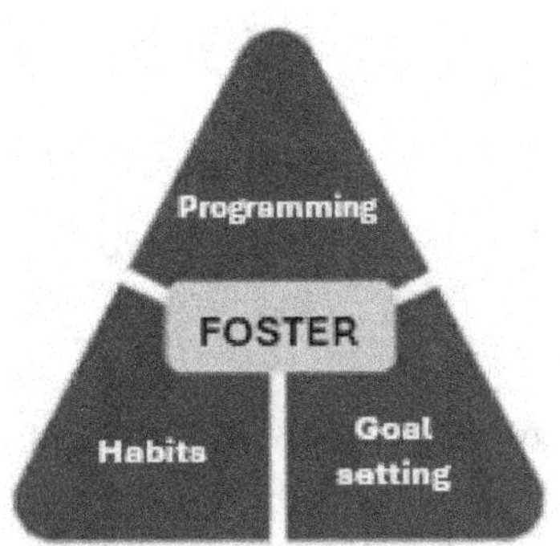

Programming
FOSTER
Habits
Goal
setting

FOSTER

The definition of FOSTER is to encourage or promote the development of (something. Typically, something regarded as good).

Fostering children during their upbringing is like tending to a delicate garden, where with care, attention, and nurturing, beautiful flowers bloom. Every interaction, every word spoken, and every gesture made shapes the trajectory of their lives. As parents, guardians, or caregivers, our role in this journey is paramount. We are not just providers of food and shelter but also architects of character, instilling values, beliefs, and a sense of belonging that will guide them throughout their lives.

One of the most significant aspects of fostering children is the opportunity to cultivate a sense of self-worth and confidence within them. By offering words of encouragement, celebrating their achievements, and providing a safe space to express themselves, we help them develop a strong sense of identity. This foundation becomes their armor as they navigate the ups and downs of life, empowering them to stand tall in the face of adversity and embrace their uniqueness with pride.

Moreover, fostering children during their upbringing lays the groundwork for building healthy relationships and fostering empathy and compassion. Through our own actions and interactions, we model kindness, respect, and understanding, teaching them the importance of treating others with dignity and empathy. By nurturing a sense of empathy within them, we cultivate future leaders who are not only capable of making a positive impact on the world but also possess the compassion to uplift those around them. In essence, fostering children is not just about raising individuals; it's about nurturing the seeds of kindness, empathy, and resilience that will blossom into a brighter future for all.

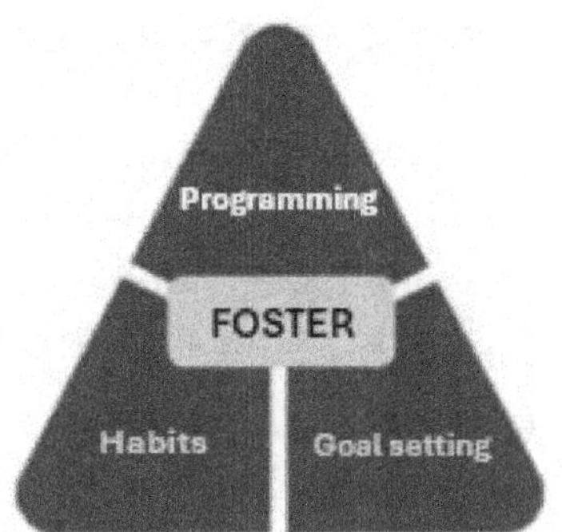

Programming
FOSTER
Habits
Goal setting

Programming

For children to have a chance at succeeding in life, they first have to be programmed to know that they can achieve whatever it is they want to. From birth until early childhood, children's minds are like a blank canvas...they have not been programed yet. "What do you mean by that?" Well, they don't know what is fact or what is fiction. They don't know what having manners means. Heck, they don't even know what manners are!

So, as parents, it is our duty to program our children with good stuff. How to speak correctly. How to sit up in their chair. How to read and write. And so on. Who else is going to teach them the basics of life? No one but us.

Programming our children with positivity is like giving them a superpower that will guide them through life's challenges with resilience and optimism. By instilling a positive mindset from an early age, we equip them with the tools to navigate the ups and downs of life with grace and determination. Whether it's through affirmations, storytelling, or leading by example, programming our children with positivity fosters a sense of confidence and self-belief that will serve as their compass in the years to come.

Moreover, programming our children in a positive manner lays the groundwork for building strong mental and emotional resilience. In a world filled with uncertainties and setbacks, a positive outlook becomes their armor, shielding them from negativity and self-doubt. By teaching them to reframe challenges as opportunities for growth and learning, we empower them to embrace life's twists and turns with courage and optimism. Through our words and actions, we sow the seeds of resilience, nurturing a generation of individuals who are not just survivors but thrivers, capable of turning setbacks into steppingstones towards a brighter future.

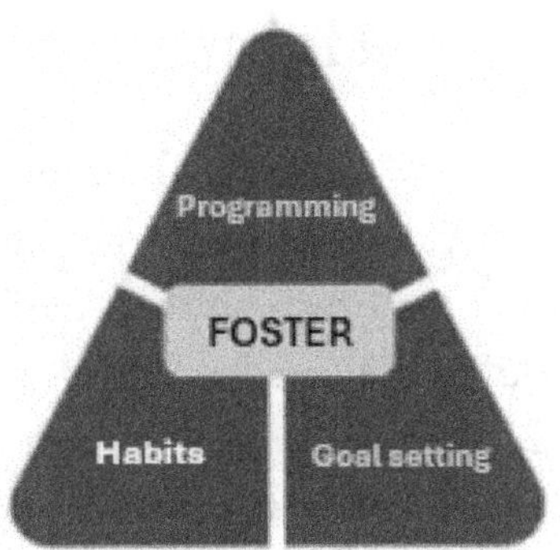
Programming
FOSTER
Habits
Goal setting

Habits

Teaching good habits to our children is like laying down the foundation for a sturdy house—it provides stability, structure, and sets them up for success in the long run. From brushing their teeth before bed to saying "please" and "thank you," these small routines may seem insignificant, but they play a crucial role in shaping their character and behavior. By instilling good habits early on, we empower our children to make positive choices that will benefit them throughout their lives.

Moreover, teaching good habits to our children promotes a sense of responsibility and accountability. By consistently reinforcing the importance of chores, time management, and personal hygiene, we help them understand the value of taking care of themselves and their surroundings. These habits not only foster independence but also instill a sense of pride in their accomplishments, laying the groundwork for a strong work ethic and a can-do attitude.

Furthermore, teaching good habits to our children cultivates a culture of respect and consideration for others. Whether it's sharing toys with siblings, holding the door open for someone, or lending a helping hand to a friend in need, these small acts of kindness ripple outwards, creating a ripple effect of positivity in the world. By modeling good behavior and teaching our children to treat others with kindness and empathy, we not only nurture their social skills but also contribute to building a more compassionate and inclusive society.

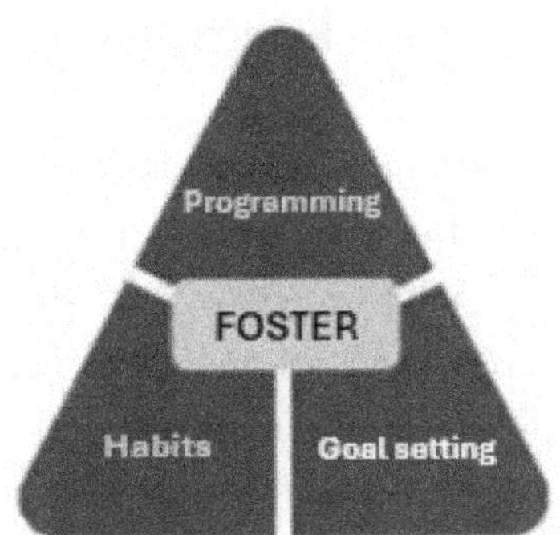
Programming
FOSTER
Habits
Goal setting

Goal setting

Teaching our children about goal setting is like handing them a treasure map to their dreams—it empowers them to navigate life with purpose, direction, and a sense of achievement. From aiming to score a goal in their soccer game to aspiring to become a scientist or an artist, setting goals provides a roadmap for turning their dreams into reality. By instilling this valuable skill from a young age, we equip our children with the tools they need to pursue their passions and unlock their full potential.

Additionally, teaching our children about goal setting fosters a sense of resilience and perseverance. Life is filled with obstacles and setbacks, but by setting clear and achievable goals, our children learn to overcome challenges with determination and resilience. Whether it's tackling a difficult math problem or facing rejection in their endeavors, the act of setting and working towards goals teaches them the importance of resilience, adaptability, and never giving up on their dreams. These lessons extend far beyond the realm of academics or extracurricular activities, shaping their mindset and approach to life's challenges with a positive outlook and a can-do attitude.

Furthermore, teaching our children about goal setting nurtures a sense of self-awareness and personal growth. By encouraging them to reflect on their strengths, weaknesses, and passions, we help them identify goals that align with their values and aspirations. As they work towards these goals, they gain a deeper understanding of themselves, their capabilities, and their potential. Through this process of self-discovery and growth, they develop confidence in their abilities and a sense of purpose that will guide them towards a fulfilling and meaningful life.

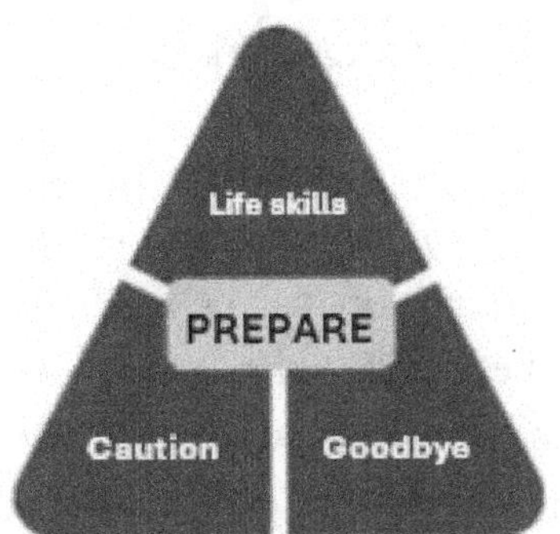
Life skills
PREPARE
Caution
Goodbye

PREPARE

Preparing our children for the day they spread their wings and leave the nest is like giving them a compass for navigating the vast sea of adulthood. As parents, our ultimate goal is to equip them with the skills, values, and resilience they need to thrive independently. From mastering basic life skills to cultivating a strong sense of self-confidence and adaptability, the journey of preparing our children for life beyond home is both rewarding and essential.

One crucial aspect of preparing our children for life away from home is teaching them practical life skills. From cooking a simple meal to managing their finances, these skills lay the foundation for self-sufficiency and independence. By involving them in household chores, budgeting exercises, and decision-making processes, we empower them to take ownership of their lives and make informed choices. Additionally, fostering open communication and providing a safe space for them to ask questions and seek guidance ensures they feel supported as they navigate the complexities of adulthood.

Lastly, preparing our children for life outside the home involves nurturing their emotional intelligence and resilience. The transition to independence can be daunting, filled with uncertainty and challenges. By teaching them coping mechanisms for stress management, problem-solving skills, and the importance of seeking help when needed, we arm them with the tools to navigate life's inevitable ups and downs. Encouraging them to embrace failure as a steppingstone towards growth and celebrating their successes, no matter how small, instills a sense of confidence and self-belief that will serve them well in their journey ahead.

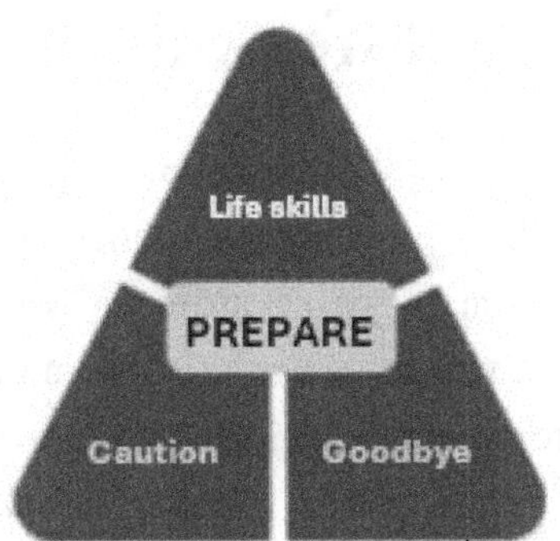

Life skills
PREPARE
Caution
Goodbye

Life skills

Life skills are the essential tools we use to navigate the world around us with confidence, resilience, and independence. They encompass a wide range of abilities that enable us to handle everyday tasks, communicate effectively, and adapt to various situations. From basic skills like cooking and cleaning to more complex abilities such as decision-making and problem-solving, life skills are the building blocks of a successful and fulfilling life.

At their core, life skills can be categorized into several key areas, including personal, social, and academic skills. Personal skills encompass self-care, time management, and organization, allowing us to prioritize tasks and maintain a healthy balance in our lives. Social skills, on the other hand, involve communication, empathy, and conflict resolution, enabling us to build meaningful relationships and navigate social interactions with ease. Academic skills, including critical thinking, research, and study techniques, are essential for success in school and beyond, equipping us with the tools to learn and grow throughout our lives.

Moreover, life skills extend beyond the practical tasks we perform and encompass qualities such as resilience, adaptability, and emotional intelligence. These traits enable us to cope with adversity, embrace change, and thrive in an ever-evolving world. By honing our life skills, we not only enhance our individual capabilities but also contribute to building stronger communities and fostering a more inclusive society. Ultimately, life skills empower us to lead fulfilling lives, pursue our passions, and overcome any obstacles that come our way with confidence and grace.

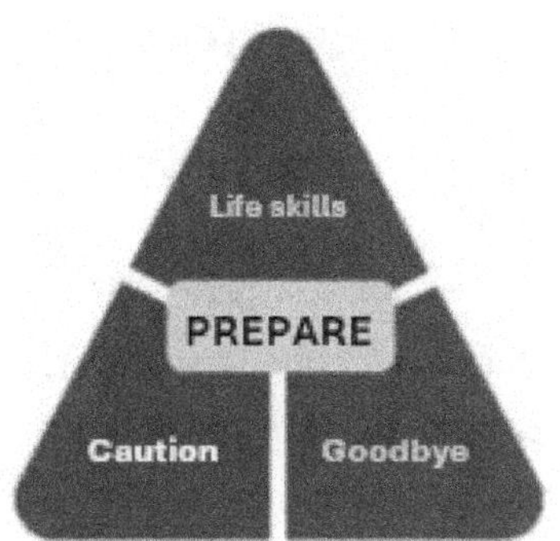
Life skills
PREPARE
Caution
Goodbye

Caution

Teaching our children to exercise caution as they navigate the complexities of adulthood is like arming them with a trusty compass for their journey. While the world is full of wonders and opportunities, it also presents its fair share of challenges and risks. As parents, it's our responsibility to equip our children with the tools they need to make informed decisions and protect themselves from harm.

One important aspect of teaching caution is instilling a sense of awareness and discernment. From an early age, we can encourage our children to trust their instincts and recognize potential dangers in their surroundings. Whether it's teaching them to look both ways before crossing the street or to be wary of strangers online, cultivating a healthy sense of caution empowers them to stay safe in various situations.

Moreover, teaching caution involves educating our children about the consequences of their actions and the importance of thinking before they act. By discussing real-life scenarios and encouraging open dialogue, we help them develop critical thinking skills and learn to weigh the risks and benefits of different choices. Whether it's resisting peer pressure, avoiding risky behaviors, or making financial decisions, teaching caution equips our children with the wisdom and resilience to navigate the ups and downs of adulthood with confidence and integrity. Through our guidance and support, they learn to tread carefully, embracing life's adventures while staying grounded in wisdom and caution.

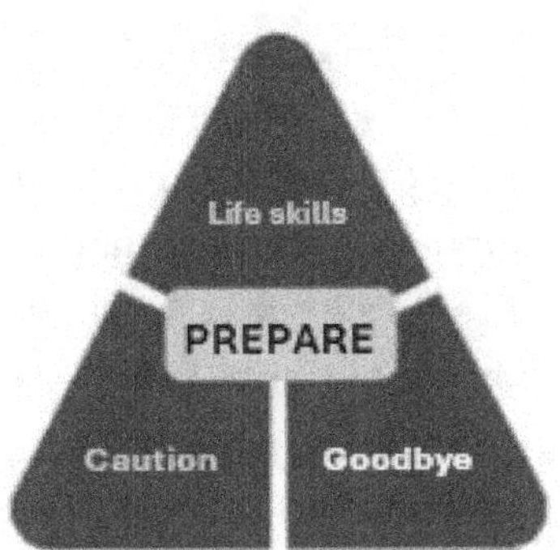
Life skills
PREPARE
Caution
Goodbye

Goodbye

The paradox of parenting is that you have spent 18 years or so nurturing and caring for your children and then you have to let them go. This was the toughest thing I had to do with my two children.

The bittersweet moment of letting our children go as they embark on their journey into young adulthood is like releasing a helium balloon into the sky—it's a mix of pride, joy, and a twinge of nostalgia. As parents, we've spent years nurturing and guiding them, preparing them to spread their wings and soar into the world. Yet, as they take their first steps towards independence, we can't help but feel a pang of sadness knowing that our roles will inevitably shift as they forge their own path.

But amidst the bittersweet emotions, there's a sense of excitement and anticipation for the adventures that lie ahead. Watching our children grow into confident, capable individuals ready to tackle the world fills us with immense pride and satisfaction. As they embark on new experiences, make their own decisions, and carve out their place in the world, we cheer them on from the sidelines, knowing that they carry with them the lessons, values, and love we've instilled in them throughout the years.

The finality of letting our children go marks a new chapter in our own lives—one of rediscovery, redefinition, and renewed purpose. With newfound freedom and space, we have the opportunity to reconnect with ourselves, pursue our passions, and embrace new experiences. While the empty nest may initially feel daunting, it also offers a chance for personal growth and fulfillment. As we bid farewell to one chapter and welcome the next, we cherish the memories we've shared, the lessons we've learned, and the love that will always bind us together, no matter where life may lead.

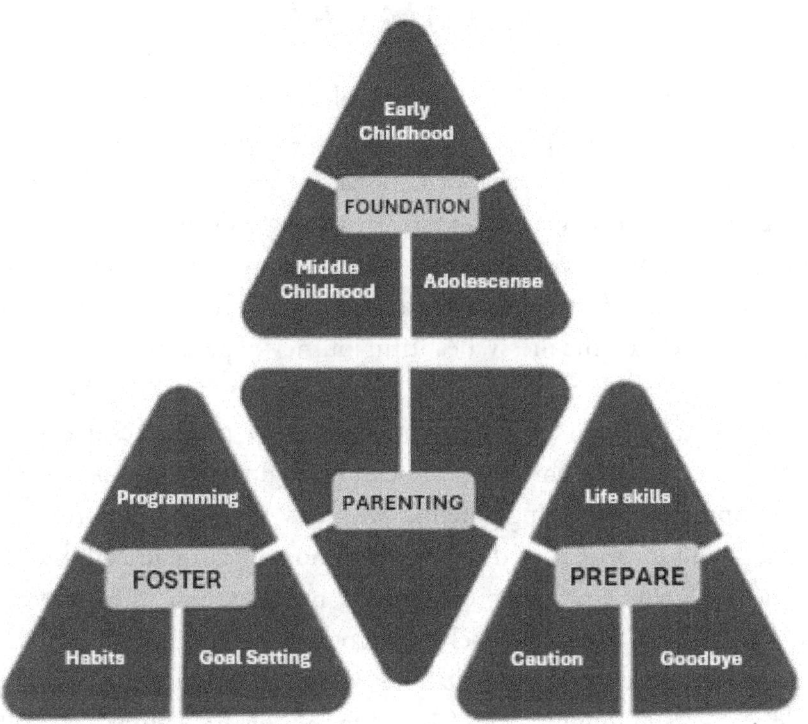
Early
Childhood
FOUNDATION
Middle
Childhood
Adolescense
Programming
PARENTING
Life skills
FOSTER
PREPARE
Habits
Goal Setting
Caution
Goodbye

SUMMARY

Parenting isn't about perfection; it's about the journey of growth, learning, and love. As parents, we strive to do our best, but we're only human, and mistakes are an inevitable part of the process. Whether it's losing our patience after a long day or making a decision that we later regret, these moments of imperfection remind us that we're all works in progress. Instead of striving for unattainable perfection, let's embrace our flaws and celebrate the messy, beautiful journey of parenthood.

In fact, our mistakes can often be our greatest teachers. When we stumble and fall, we have the opportunity to model resilience and perseverance for our children. By acknowledging our mistakes, taking responsibility, and making amends, we show them the importance of humility and integrity. It's through these moments of vulnerability that we demonstrate the value of growth mindset and the power of forgiveness, both towards ourselves and others.

Moreover, parenting is a collaborative effort, and we don't have to do it alone. Seeking support from friends, family, or professionals can offer valuable perspective and guidance along the way. Whether it's swapping stories with other parents, attending parenting workshops, or seeking therapy when needed, reaching out for help is a sign of strength, not weakness. Together, let's create a community where we can share our triumphs and struggles, knowing that we're all in this journey of parenthood together, imperfectly perfect, and always learning along the way.

Invitation

It's funny. When you're in the middle of parenting there are ups and downs as well as laughter and frustrations. It's exhausting to work a full-time job and raise children at the same time! There's very little "me" time as I recall. Now looking back 25 years ago, I seem to only remember the good times of parenting. I had such a blast raising my two kids that I was tempted to do it again. But alas, parenting requires lots of energy! So as an older person, I surrendered to the fact that my child-rearing days were behind me.

I said all of that to say this: there are days where you'll wonder how you're going to continue to parent without losing your mind. Lots of chaos and on the go all the time wears on a parent's patience. Well, the truth is...parenting is a 20-year commitment. It has to take priority over everything else in order to do a good job of raising children.

The time is going to come when your children have left the nest and you will wonder "Where did the time go?" and you will begin to reminisce about the last 20 years. Over time, you will forget the tough times and only remember the good times. It's crazy but that's really what happens.

So, I invite you to give yourself a break...by taking a break. Once in a while (and you'll know when!), you'll need to just get away and have some "me" time. That's not being selfish, that's being healthy. Decompressing with some R&R is necessary along the way.

Also, don't beat yourself up if things are not going perfectly. There will be storms of life and somehow, we find a way to navigate around those issues. When it's all over, you'll look back and say "I'm glad I became a parent" and go have a glass of wine. You accomplished one of the greatest privileges in life...raising kids.

When you're with someone who is sharing their struggles with you...just smile at him/her and give them one of these. He/she will ask "What is that?" Then simply reply "Life Works in Threes."

Other titles coming out:

- Weight Struggles?
- Abundance Struggles?
- Life Struggles?
- Romance Struggles?
- Purpose Struggles?
- Happiness Struggles?
- Sales Struggles?
- Speaker Struggles?
- Time Struggles?
- Network Struggles?
- Marriage Struggles?
- Divorce Struggles?
- Money Struggles?
- Career Struggles?
- Dating Struggles?
- Caretaker Struggles?
- Forgiveness Struggles?
- Grieving Struggles?
- Success Struggles?
- Golf Struggles?
- Workplace Struggles?
- Stress Struggles?
- Shame/Guilt Struggles?
- Addiction Struggles?

Quotes about Parenting

"Parenting is about guiding the future, not controlling it." - Unknown

"Parenting is the biggest sacrifice one can make, it's putting your life on hold to fulfill the promise of your children's tomorrow." - Wes Fessler

"The best kind of parent you can be...is to lead by example." - Drew Barrymore

"Your children need your presence more than your presents." - Jesse Jackson

"There is no such thing as a perfect parent. So just be a real one." - Sue Atkins

Here are some characteristics or traits in **boys** that parents might want to be aware of:

1. **Physical Activity**: Many boys tend to be highly active and may require outlets for their energy.
2. **Risk-Taking Behavior**: Boys often exhibit a tendency towards risk-taking and adventurous activities.
3. **Competitiveness**: There's often a strong desire to compete, whether in sports, academics, or other areas.
4. **Emotional Expression**: Boys may express emotions differently than girls, sometimes struggling with articulating feelings.
5. **Independence**: A growing desire for independence and autonomy can be common.
6. **Social Dynamics**: Boys may navigate friendships and social hierarchies with a different approach than girls.
7. **Interest in Gadgets and Technology**: Generally, there's a strong attraction to gadgets, video games, and technology.
8. **Interest in Physical Play**: Roughhousing and physical play are often preferred methods of interaction.
9. **Communication Style**: Communication patterns might lean towards being more direct and action-oriented.
10. **Learning Styles**: Learning preferences can vary, with some boys excelling in hands-on activities or visual learning.

It's important to note that these characteristics can vary widely among individuals, and not all boys will exhibit every trait listed. Understanding these tendencies can help parents better support their child's development and navigate potential challenges effectively.

Here are some characteristics or traits in girls that parents might want to be aware of:

1. **Verbal Skills**: Girls often develop verbal and language skills earlier and may have a larger vocabulary.
2. **Social Sensitivity**: There's often a heightened awareness of social dynamics and relationships.
3. **Emotional Expression**: Girls may express a wide range of emotions more openly and verbally.
4. **Cooperation and Collaboration**: Girls tend to emphasize cooperation and collaboration in social interactions.
5. **Attention to Detail**: There's often a tendency towards paying attention to details in activities and relationships.
6. **Empathy**: Girls often display empathy towards others' feelings and emotions.
7. **Interest in Relationships**: There may be a stronger interest in maintaining and nurturing friendships.
8. **Creativity**: Girls often demonstrate creativity in various forms, such as arts, storytelling, or imaginative play.
9. **Organization**: There's often a preference for organized environments and routines.
10. **Communication Style**: Communication patterns might lean towards discussing emotions and building rapport.

As with boys, these characteristics can vary widely among individuals, and not all girls will exhibit every trait listed. Understanding these tendencies can help parents better support their child's development and build a strong parent-child relationship.

Remember,
When you get right down to it,
Life is about making choices.
Every day, all day long, that's what we do.

- *We choose to get out of bed or not.*
- *We choose to clean up or not.*
- *We choose what to eat all day.*
- *We choose to exercise or not.*
- *We choose to go to work or not.*
- *We choose to do a good job or not.*
- *We choose to come home or not.*
- *We choose to watch TV or do something constructive.*
- *We choose to bed at a decent hour or not.*

And the next day...we start all over again.

What is the meaning of this? Get good at choosing.

Before you can get good at choosing though...you need to understand how life works in threes.

When someone is struggling with a particular area or two, chances are they are "out of balance" with how life works. How does life work? Life works in threes.

If you're interested in personal topics like life, health, money or business topics like sales, time management and public speaking...TRYUNE WORKS! can shed some light on creating success in those areas.

The definition of TRIUNE is a group of three things; united. Being three in one, such as - humans are *mental, physical* and *spiritual beings*. The word TRYUNE is a play of the word TRIUNE, encouraging all to try this concept and help eliminate struggling unnecessarily.

LifeWorksInThrees.com

www.ingramcontent.com/pod-product-compliance
Lightning Source LLC
Chambersburg PA
CBHW061632130726
47996CB00003B/1246